Arthur and Esther

A Play For Two Soloists

Ross Howard

A SAMUEL FRENCH ACTING EDITION

FOUNDED 1830

SAMUELFRENCH.COM
SAMUELFRENCH-LONDON.CO.UK

MUSIC USE NOTE

IMPORTANT BILLING AND CREDIT REQUIREMENTS

ARTHUR AND ESTHER was first produced at The Studio at Cherry Lane Theatre, New York on 21st August 2007. The performance was directed by Sarah Norris with lighting by David Diaz. The cast was as follows:

ARTHUR . . . . Taylor Hanes

This version of the play was first produced at the Onyx Theatre, Las Vegas, on 9th November 2012. The performance was directed by Brandon Burk with lighting by Jake Copenhaver, set by Michael Morse and David Sankuer and music by Zoë Kohen Ley. The cast was as follows:

ARTHUR . . . . Taylor Hanes
ESTHER . . . . .Breon Jenay

CHARACTERS

ARTHUR HUEY – Long-serving community librarian. Mid 50s.
ESTHER HUEY – His wife in life. Eternally youthful. Mid 20s.

SCENE

A low lit, empty library in the north-west of England and a brightly lit area somewhere in the afterlife.

ACKNOWLEDGEMENTS

Jerry L. Crawford, Sarah Norris, Jim Amstutz, Becky Coleman, Jakob Holder, Quinn M. Corbin, Oscar F. Limon, Dana Martin, Brandon Burk, Anthony Del Valle, Glenn Casale, Jayme McGhan, Lisa Easley, Timothy Trimingham Lee, Jeff Martin, Timothy Daly, Bruce Pachtman, Charles O' Connor, Mark Muro, Peter Corkhill, Jensen Mabe, Marcel Nunis, Renee Newlove, Tom Atkinson, Stephen Barnett, Nadia Papachronopoulou, Antonia Reid, Geoff Leesley and Violet Patton-Ryder.

This play is dedicated to Taylor Hanes

and to Mum and Dad

ARTHUR AND ESTHER

(A low light up on **ARTHUR**. *He sits behind a table with an old sports bag to one side of him and a litre bottle of water on the other.)*

ARTHUR. Long lost patrons. Loyal to the last. You catch me in a point of fall. *(He unzips the sports bag and begins to rummage through it.)* Things have...capsized. If you can grasp my meaning. But to continue...and establish things...in an accurate manner, I must make it clear that I am not "lost at sea". No not at all. Nor do I feel like I'm "up the creek without a paddle". *(His rummaging increases with purpose.)* It's important I think... I think it's important to get your metaphors in order. Water related or otherwise. *(He pulls out a tub of paracetamol. He studies the label.)*

ESTHER. *(in the darkness, she speaks in a rapid tempo, a heightened sort of monotone)* In over your head, out of your depth, heavy, so, so heavy, pushing, pushing down, pulling you down, push— heavy again, very heavy, heavy, light, light now, light, feeling light, light, dark, darker, darker, black.

ARTHUR. Things are bad, have gone bad...but I do know where I am. By God, I do know that. It's what to do next...or rather how. *(He attempts to open the tub but somehow is unable to do so.)*

(Bright lights up on **ESTHER**. *They are almost blinding at first. She looks down at herself, what she is wearing. She looks at her hands with a sort of wonder, she touches her face, runs them down her body etc.)*

ESTHER. Where are we now? Look at me. Look at you. Who are you? Crikey, look at...my hands! *(She grabs her backside. She smacks her backside. She looks down at her* *breasts.)* Well! This place is different! So who are you, seriously? Sorry, blimmin' 'eck. I mean, hello. Hi, what are your names? So we've moved. Why've we moved? You seem a little, I don't know, little nervous. You know really don't be, it's fine honestly – yeah, yeah, no, me too. I'm nervous. Where are we?

ARTHUR. I do know where I am. By God, I do know that. It's what to do next…or rather how. I've already decided what I'm going to do. As for why…well I just want to have my say first. And somebody to listen. *(He bangs the tub on the edge of the table.)* They're closing my library and I'm going to kill myself. *(He again tries to open it more forcefully but is just as unsuccessful.)* On deciding the method, one of the perks of being a librarian…and of a library, has always been that information – on any given thing I might add – is always right there under your nose. Now with the internet, they say it's all at your fingertips. People seem to be getting lazier and lazier. The joy of searching for something and finding it, like you're a…persistent detective trying to crack a case…that's…gone. I foresee a time when everyone will just have wires stuck on to their head, wires trailing behind them as they walk, and every thought process they might have or question they have will be answered immediately by a supersonic electronic boost. A cocktail of megabytes, volts and megawatts surging into the brain and PDF, MP3, zip-zap documents opening with a flickering, scrolling speed. Accompanied by the flashing pop up box telling you you've won a yacht. So congratulations for thinking. Or thinking about thinking. *(He reads the label on the tub.)* I sound… I know. But civilization is crumbling. *(He takes out a pair of glasses from the top pocket of his shirt under the sweater.)*

ESTHER. It's been like this from the start, don't you think? No explanations. Just to wait. You can say a little something. It's okay, really. Anything? So why *are you* here? What did *you* do? *(A beat)* Wait, wait, wait. I asked once, I said, "Are we in Purgatory or something?" but they just smiled at me all condescending like I was asking if Father Christmas and his reindeer had been here yet. I think they also thought I was being ungrateful and were kind of offended. Well he did. Thingumybob. He looked like he was put out a little. You know the one I'm talking about? Looks a bit like Burt Reynolds from that movie *White Lightning*? Everyone else just comes and goes but he's the only one I really see all the time. Where was he before, I wonder? He's the one I always see. I nearly asked him if he was God once but I thought that after the whole Purgatory thing it could get round here that I'd gone crackers. *(A beat)* Besides, he seems more like he's in the administration side of things. But eh, just imagine. *That he was God.* What an anti-climax, I'm just saying. But I mean, he's handsome. If you like that kind of thing, I suppose. And most people do. Funny.

ARTHUR. My father used to say "Melvil" – that wasn't my name but when my father spoke you listened – "Melvil, there is nothing like the smell of a book." *(He puts his glasses on and immediately takes them off.)* And I think he's right. My father loved books and kept a respectable library at home as well as the one he kept here between these four walls. *(He wipes the glasses with his sleeve, breathes on them and polishes.)* At the dinner table we would quiz him on the opening line of any literary masterpiece you can think of and he would recite it word perfect. But just weeks before he died he confessed that he had only read the opening *two* pages of every great novel written in the English language and never went beyond. *(He puts the glasses on and pushes them to the end of his nose.)* I admitted to him that on nights I couldn't sleep I would sneak downstairs for something to eat and catch him systematically bending the spines in four different places of his newly delivered paperbacks and putting them on the shelves giving them the look of having been read. *(He reads the* *top of the cap of the paracetamol tub.)* He apologised and just asked me not to tell Mother. I never did. But when I visit his grave from time to time and read the epitaph which my mum suggested, it breaks my heart… "Here lies Alvin Frank Huey 1926-1987. Loving husband to Mary. Loving father to Arthur. He lived his life cover to cover." *(Silence)*

ESTHER. So come on, where the hell are we? I know we're not *in* Hell. I mean you all look great! *(Silence)* You're welcome. And me too. *(Touches her face)* I mean, I can tell, and the food here's cracking! And eh, come on, we don't really have to lift a finger, do we? I mean, in some ways, we've come up trumps. It's also quite temperate for another thing and there's no blasting furnace or senseless whippings or anything like that. So it's not Hell. You know what I'm on about. No one's running around wailing and tearing at their hair or raping and torturing the new arrivals or anything like that, are they? No forced sing-alongs. I mean, can you imagine? Crikey. But maybe that's on the other wing. Who knows? *(A beat)* You don't, do you? I mean you can tell me.

ARTHUR. But back to the…of where I was going. Where I started. The method. Since it was published in 1982, we have had a book in the library, *28 Ways to Terminate Your Existence and Questions You May Have* by Montgomery Swank. A Canadian. ISBN 0453527941. We kept it in our "Personal Development" section at first. *(He slowly and precisely turns the cap of the paracetamol.)* It's a well-known book among librarians as we frequently have to re-order it. For reasons you would imagine. It's seldom returned once checked out. Testimony to the accuracy of the content, I suppose. *(He opens the tub with an unnecessary force and the paracetamol shoot out. He prowls the floor collecting the pills, wiping them on his sleeve and putting them back into the tub.)* We later kept it under "Restricted Use". I wouldn't regard myself as a penny pincher – it's just one book – nevertheless, it all adds up. Just out of curiosity and given the history we had with that particular book, I would monitor what kind of people would be looking at it. Mostly it was medical students and the like, which I thought was all innocent enough. You did get others who seemed to have more of a vested interest, but it wasn't my place to interfere. I never felt right about that kind of thing. *(He takes two paracetamol with water.)* But anyway, when they told me of their plans to close the library they offered me a settlement and said I could keep as many books as I had room for at home. For some reason, I could only think of the Swank book and I took it home with me that night. They came by yesterday and boxed everything up and today they took everything away. They left me the keys so I could say goodbye to the carpet and windows and then I'm to lock up and switch the lights off, they said. *(He reaches into the sports bag and pulls out a petrol can and a large box of matches.)*

ESTHER. They don't tell us anything. It's not like it's bad here, I mean don't think I'm complaining but you can tell we're in a different place now, that's all I'm saying. Like something really amazing is going on just over there somewhere and we're stuck here. Somewhere just nearby. Like you can hear it, feel it, smell it almost. Up on the next floor or across the river or what have you. It's just a feeling you get, you know? Almost like we're in Birkenhead. You know? With Liverpool just over there in the distance. I don't know, I've never spent much time in that neck of the woods if truth be told. Merseyside. But I once went to a pottery class and there was a lady who was from there and she wasn't all that bad really and she said it was alright. So I suppose when I put it like that it comes highly recommended. *(A beat)* I know Southport of course. Formby. They're not Blackpool. But that's just me. I don't know where you stand on all that. The Battle of the Beaches. As nobody calls it. No, this is not Hell. Can't be. It just doesn't have that...*ambience*. No. So where are you all from? Geographically speaking? You know, it's so cosmopolitan here, if people spoke to one another I think we'd really learn a lot about things.

ARTHUR. "Huey" as a last name came solely from my father. Our family name is Dewey, which is an influential name in the development of libraries across the United States of America. My great-grandfather is Melvil Dewey. If you have heard of the Dewey Decimal Classification System, well that was his idea. He came up with it when working as an assistant librarian at university over there. He was only there for three years, and that's what he did while he was there. So you could say we have libraries in the blood in our family.

ESTHER. Just no children here. Strange. I sort of miss them. It must be just a life on earth kind of thing, kids. Makes sense, I suppose. We never had children, Arthur and I. I mean, I couldn't, you know. Or he couldn't. Or something. One of the two anyway, or both. I mean, they could never really tell us why. That library, that was *his* baby. *(A beat)* If I could do it all again, I'd have been a mother. We'd have made that happen somehow. I'd have made sure about that. A boy would have been just cracking. He'd have been a little smasher. Maybe two boys. A pair of sons. Daughters are all well and good, but, well there's all kinds of things that can go wrong or happen to daughters. They grow up so fast. Especially these days. Down there. But sons – as long as they stay out of prison they'll be just fine really. *(A beat)* Something the both of you can share and invest in. Something together. Keep the whole planet ticking along. Human beings with your physical likeness, you know, just walking around on earth, swinging arms gently in the pouring rain…or even just standing there looking all serious, eating an apple or what have you. Maybe they'd have liked waving to strangers. Not like they were – like they weren't with it, you know. I just

mean they'd have been real friendly types. Eh, they'd
have been right little belters.

ARTHUR. Great-grandfather Dewey also helped found the
community of Lake Placid too. During their Great
Depression his son, Godfrey, my grandfather, was
president of the organizing committee of the 1932
Winter Olympics which were to take place there.
He donated some of the family land to be used for
construction of a bobsleigh run. It was then that the
two-crew event as we now know it was introduced.
*(He unscrews the top of the petrol can, sniffs the contents
and grimaces. He screws the top back on.)* Despite being
born into such circles, my father wanted to be exposed
to more and at the age of nineteen went to Europe,
defeated Hitler, found himself in Lancashire carrying
a slight limp and a smuggled German officer pistol,
and met my mum at a bus stop. She was a Roget. As in
the thesaurus. And the Dewey family were delighted
with the prospect of uniting with the Rogets. Two
of the great families in the history of reference.
But my mother's family were all mill workers from
Ramsbottom, partially illiterate and no relation. With
the very real threat of disownment from the Dewey
family once they found out, my father changed his last
name to Huey, married my mother and they stayed
right here. He took the community library position
here. When I was old enough I became his assistant.
When he died, I was captain of the whole ship. Until
last week.

ESTHER. They'd have been right little smashers. I'm sure
of that. Still, it's not everything. And it's really no
excuse when it comes down to it and no one can say
for sure if that would have changed things any. And
I really did try to keep things going for the both of
us… "keep things going"… I mean, I don't mean
it was as bad as all that, I mean me and Arthur, well
we're talking about twenty-nine years. I just mean I'd
do things because I loved him. I *still* love him. Even

from here. Do you think that's... I don't know... I long
for him. I do. Almost to the point of craving, really.
Silly old craving. That's probably not very Women's
Lib of me to admit, is it? But I do, I really miss him.
The immense, quiet distance between us both. Makes
my stomach turn. I do wonder how he is and what he's
doing. You do, don't you? *(A silence)* You're not much
into your conversation, are you?

ARTHUR. I perhaps should have seen it coming when they
renamed it an "Academic Centre" eighteen months
ago. It was always a library to me but that was the
best compromise because apparently it could have
been even worse. The young man who oversaw the
installation of the dozen or so computers we had
delivered told me that they initially came up with the
idea of renaming it "The Info Lounge".

ESTHER. You're more into the listening side of things. I see.
Well, that's fine. Here's a story. One evening Arthur
came home complaining that they had just installed
four new computers over there at the library. They
had put them right opposite his front desk and that
he had to look at those screens with the flashing logo
moving up and down and from side to side, dancing
and bouncing around, saving the screen or something.
Screen savers. He found it very distracting. Anyway,
the next day at dawn, while he was still fast asleep, I
crept out of bed and drove down there and let myself
in. I had found out from Tina and Tom at my work
that you could have anything you wanted on there,
whatever you typed it would flash it for you, bounce
it around from side to side and the screen would still
be saved and everything. So that's what I did. I typed
"You are loved, Esther". I slowed it down too so he
couldn't miss it. Sure enough it would have been there
when he opened later. On all four computers, just
yards opposite him. He really had to have seen it. But
he didn't say anything about it when he got back that
night and by the next day when I brought him lunch it
had been taken off.

ARTHUR. In the first chapter of the book Swank talks about setting yourself on fire. "Self immolation". Which sounds absolutely terrifying. I thought it was an odd one to begin with as it seems pretty much the most violent of ways to go. You'd have thought he would have saved that for the end…only for those who found the previous methods and chapters just not their cup of tea and really wanted to go out in a blaze of… well, a blaze. *(He opens the box of matches, takes one out and strikes it. He watches it burn as he speaks.)* Seems a real kind of a statement on how you…how you go about things and if I ever learned of anyone I knew do this, I'd have thought they must be feeling pretty bad about themselves. But reading what Swank says it supposedly signifies some kind of protest…and that really got to me for a second. Is that what I am doing? Because I hate what they've done, yes – I've got to say it put me in a real bind, because I suppose I am in a way. Protesting. But like I said, the idea of engulfing myself in flames gives me kittens. And that's the truth. *(The match burns out. Silence. He puts the burnt match(es) back in the box and closes it. He pushes both the box of matches and the petrol can out of his reach.)* It would have been a wonder if that had worked out anyway. Even if I did what you were supposed to. I never was able to get a fire going. I can't explain it. I just never had the ability to get that particular element to obey me. Barbeques down the years were always somebody else's handywork. I'd just sit there and hand them the meat. "Throw another log on the fire, Melvil!" my dad would yell and next moment everyone would be rubbing their eyes and coughing as the fire went out and the smoke went everywhere. They say "there's no smoke without fire" – well, whoever started saying that obviously never spent May bank holiday with the Hueys, I can tell you that. Smoke was about it really when I had a go. *(He takes two paracetamol with water.)* It seems a little thing. Not being good at something like that but when it stays with you into your adult years…

then it stops being funny, stops being cute...it nags
at you a little. It becomes a weakness you get a little
insecure about. My wife and I. My ex wife. My only
wife. Esther. She really liked camping. A real outdoors
kind of girl she was. She hiked, climbed, all that kind
of thing. We used to go camping up in the Lake
District. Just she and I – and a good friend of mine,
Richard. Or "Dick" as I used to call him. I was the only
one he'd let call him "Dick". We were like two peas in
a pod, he and I. He worked at the local museum. He
lost his wife on a visit to Egypt. Very sad. She was a big
lady and got stuck in one of those little tunnels they
have in the pyramids over there. It was during one of
those guided tours they put on. She panicked and had
some kind of attack. Dick was crestfallen as you can
imagine. So for the next few years after that Esther and
I really took Dick under our wing. He'd sometimes
drop by and help me with the stacks in the evening,
and then we'd walk home together and Esther would
always have a dinner place set for him and really put
on a spread. She was an excellent cook, my wife. One
of the best. But Dick could certainly get a fire going
and he always showed me up on those camping trips,
the tinker. It sounds daft, I know. The man's wife died
and here I was jealous of him! Like somehow he was
impressing my wife with what he could do and what
I couldn't! But he really came into his own on those
camping trips and I think we really snapped him out
of a pretty bad spell. The last time we went up there
as the "Three Musketeers" was the weekend of my
fiftieth birthday. Each time before that, we always got
the same weather up there. We were never caught in
the rain. Blue skies, sun sprinkling through the trees.
Always the same. The sound of children playing,
the smell of campfires and sausages. I was never an
outdoors kinda fella but it really grew on me if you
want to know the truth. Although that last weekend.
That weekend was very strange. It was like we were
the last three people on earth. The weather. Didn't

rain, didn't shine…it just kinda sat. No breeze. You couldn't hear a sound. All I could hear were those two laughing at each other's jokes. They really clicked in the sense of humour department, Esther and Dick. It really made those weekends work in a way. It was never a case of him being a third wheel or anything like that. But that was all there was to hear on that particular weekend. As for the smell…all my nostrils could get a whiff of, all I could smell was his damn Old Spice or whatever he wore. *(He laughs.)* Old Dick with his Old Spice…and her perfume. She wasn't a stranger to throwing it on either. Made you wonder if she swam in the stuff but I was always polite about it. But the Old Spice and the perfume. Sometimes you would get a mixture of the two. Like they both merged into just one smell *(He laughs.)* I thought, "Crikey, they've even got their own smell between them". By about Saturday afternoon, I had figured it out. Right there going on under my nose and I hadn't even suspected. That weekend I gave her a couple of tests. Just a couple of times. Maybe I'd walk twenty or so yards away, a thoughtful stroll, wait to see if she followed me. Ask me what was wrong or what I was thinking. But she never did. She just stayed with him. Making jokes. Watching him put more wood on the fire. As it burned away. They told me what they wanted me to know as we were driving back that Sunday evening and by the following Wednesday they both came to see me here at the library to say their goodbyes to me and let me know they were moving to Cheshire. They seemed to think it was all for the best and it's hard to argue when it's put like that and the decision's been made without you. Not a lot you can really do. I don't know…too often you're a casualty of other people's opinion of progress. *(He takes two paracetamol with water.)*

ESTHER. Richard, or "Dick" as Arthur used to call him. He'd only let Arthur call him "Dick". Well, it was harmless at first. I mean it just sort of developed like I suppose

things do. Richard was very good at persuading other
museums, mainly those Natural History ones, much
bigger ones, to loan them their exhibits from time to
time. Just for a month or so he was able to have them,
and sometimes he would need help setting up. That
was all. Arthur was always too busy to help him during
the day and so Richard would ask me to come down
and lend a hand. It felt good to be asked, you know?
Well there were all kinds of things he would have
down there. It was a real treasure trove. Arthur never
asked for my help at the library and with all that time
to myself and Richard inviting me down there, well it
got me out of the house. One day I get a phone call.
It's Richard telling me about this new anthropology
display that had just arrived and he asked me to come
down and see. He sounded so excited. These were the
men in my life. Libraries and museums. You couldn't
make it up really. Well anyway, when I got down there
he opened the door and he was all made up looking
like one of those *Homo erectus* types, a caveman, you
know? Just a bit of a cloth covering his cash and prizes
but all the rest of him as naked as the day he was born,
oh it was funny. He did make me laugh. He closed up
for the afternoon and chased me around the museum
for a couple of hours with a spear. *(A beat)* We were like
two kids that day and days like that started to happen
more and more. He was just a lot of fun. The first time
he kissed me, I remember, was in a fibreglass igloo.
We were just messing around being two Eskimos. We
started rubbing our noses together just being silly
and that's when he kissed me. Well that's when the
floodgates opened and there was just no way back
after that. Days like the Eskimos would happen more
or less every day from then on. And there was always
a reason I could think of to go down to the museum
and if I couldn't think of one, Richard did. *(A beat)*
We were disgusting really, when I think about it. The
way we went about all that. We didn't think we were at
the time as much, but we were. See, you get yourself

into a situation like that, at that stage of your life and you begin to see it as an opportunity more than anything. And the thought of not taking it is the thing that scares you the most. When you're in that frame of mind you just do it, I suppose. And when you're attracted to something you're attracted to something, it's not so much of a choice. What's common sense, right or wrong, that goes right out the window.

ARTHUR. I still had my library however, and we had just begun an afternoon reading group for eight-year-olds and under in that particular week which all in all turned out to be quite successful. So much so that those Thursday afternoon sessions with the kids continued right up until last week – before the vultures came in. A whole seven years we ran that group, and that's three and a half years longer than those two lasted together, I hear. Dick had got busy with some project or other...teaching a chimpanzee at Chester Zoo how to play table tennis or something and had devoted himself to that though the results were not what he had hoped, and Esther, she drowned herself in a lake. I intended to go to the funeral but could never get out of the car when it came time to go in. I turned the radio on and looked for a parking spot near the cemetery. I stayed long enough to see them lower the coffin and then I pulled away. Dick wasn't there either. Apparently, in those recent months he could be seen around town wrapped from head to toe in tinfoil and that coupled with the monkey experiments led his cousin to come up from Ipswich and take him away. I can't imagine what Esther would have made of it all...well I can...but I wonder why she chose to do that. They never married. She could have found somebody else. She just never seemed the type, that's all I'm saying. It doesn't give me any satisfaction the way all that turned out, I don't like to think about any of it if you really need to know, but that's the way it goes, I suppose.

ESTHER. You really couldn't say there was a winner in that whole situation. What with Richard going cuckoo and me and Arthur belly-up. I think Richard's wife got the best of it probably. I wonder where she went after Egypt. I'm always on the lookout for certain folk I knew who popped their clogs but I haven't seen anyone I recognise. You know, she seemed really nice the times the two of them came over for dinner at Arthur's and mine. Before she went with Richard to Egypt on their trip of a lifetime and died. She was very...bubbly, I always remember thinking that. And she made her own pâté that you would've killed for. It was out of this world. Or that world. Truly. Delicious. Though you know I always knew that size of hers was going be the death of her. I mean I couldn't have guessed that it would've happened precisely the way it did. Who could have guessed something like that? All those sunburned folk in shorts and sandals watching you struggle as your big ol' behind is wedged in between the – or however it went...just awful. Poor Richard. I mean, really. Poor guy. But blimmin' 'eck, did I live in the shadow of that woman! Richard and I were both sitting on the new sofa one afternoon, if you can picture that, the first thing we bought together, watching the History Channel or whatever it was. Sitting on the sofa on a Sunday afternoon watching a documentary which he always liked to do when suddenly they get to talking about that old Tutankhamun. Richard just, well, he didn't even make an attempt to conceal it, the daft 'apeth. He starts blubbing like a baby!

ARTHUR. For some reason, Swank's chapter on drowning was one of the hardest to read in the book. There was Esther obviously, I wouldn't lie to you – she was running through my mind a lot as I was going through – she did what she did, yes – but you don't like to think of someone you know who...you know.

ESTHER. There I am sitting there on our brand new three-piece Persian leather sofa we had just bought that very morning...me the one who had left a twenty-nine year marriage for the man sitting right next to me, and the sight of some ancient death chambers and the talk of embalming techniques on the telly gets him thinking and remembering and crying about his ex-wife! Wailing into his hanky!

ARTHUR. But the other thing is, it gets pretty technical, the chapter. And the more scientific it got the more gruesome the whole thing began to sound. Worse than setting yourself on fire in many ways. Or at least as bad. That's what it seemed. Lots of talk of oxygen being prevented...carbon dioxide flushing out, air tubes, airways, blockages, a lot of lung talk. Words like hypoxia, hypocapnia, hyperventilation. And I've never liked the word "submerge". Just never have. So I never considered it an option really. *(He pulls out some rope from the sports bag and ties a noose.)*

ESTHER. I offered him a chocolate and that just set him off some more. It was Toblerone, you know? I don't know, I wasn't thinking, and offering him pyramid-shaped chocolates perhaps wasn't the best idea given the circumstances. *(A beat)* Now all that later with him covering the house with cling film and the smoke detectors with his socks, hiding in the wardrobe wrapped in tinfoil thinking we were being watched, well I can't explain that.

ARTHUR. But going back to Esther, I...er...there's... something I have been thinking about...something that's crossed my mind about...all of this. And it worries me greatly. I'm not a religious man... I mean it's been donkeys' years since I...but I did speak before God and I did take my vows seriously and solemnly on our wedding day. I meant it all. I couldn't have guessed what was actually going to happen. But...but I do believe that when we pass we join up with the ones that went before us. I do believe that. The ones closest. And, well I fear that. I fear they're going to pair me up with her again. For eternity. And that's a long time. In anyone's book. *(He takes two paracetamol with water.)* We never actually signed anything, you see. You know, to end it once and for all. I don't even think she even went back to her maiden name. So I suppose in a way we're still married... I'm pretty sure she did what she did that night up at the lake...while still under the name Mrs. Arthur Huey. And up there, I can't see how it would have changed. It will still be there on a scrap of paper somewhere, and when I'm at the gates or the turnstile or what have you, they'll look down at the list and give me the keys to Room 506 and say "Your wife's waiting for you" and I'll say "No, there must be some mistake" and the bloke will raise his eyebrows all funny and say "Do you know where you are, sir?" and I'll say "Yes, it's Heaven" and he'll say back, in a condescending manner "Yes, it's Heaven." And we'll look at each other and then he'll look down at his clipboard and tap it. "I don't know what you've been told, but we don't make mistakes up here" and then I'll tell him that I understand all that, but there were developments that they might not be aware of. And then he'll look over at someone else in the vicinity as if to say "We have a real character here". And I'll do my best to ignore it, and tell them about Dick, and the camping and the afternoon they came in to see me at the library, and he'll just say something like "So she is not your wife? She is not Mrs Arthur Huey?" and I'll say "Well, yes, she is...but what I'm trying to tell you—" and he'll interrupt and say "We do have other people waiting, sir. Whatever was down there is not up here. Room 506. She's waiting" and I'll say "No, where's my father? Let me speak to my father" and he'll snap back "All in good time. Now move along" and I'll say "Melvil Dewey! Tell me where Melvil Dewey is. I want to speak to him!" and that would really stir something up inside him and he'll come back with "Melvil Dewey invented *the* method in which we classify and categorize any large collection of manuscripts in any one given place!" And I would reply "Yes! And bravo!" but he won't be having any of it and he'll just sneer "What business is it of yours to see him immediately on arrival?" and I'll say "He's my great-grandfather" and he'll say "But you're a Huey. He's a Dewey. How can that possibly be the case?" And I'll tell him about Grandpa Godfrey and Lake Placid and the Winter Olympics of 1932, and when Dad came over here and met Mum and he'll start to walk away muttering something about me spinning him a line, and I'll say "With respect, I really think you should be more open-minded. I think you're a narrow thinker if you want to know the truth." and that would really do it and he'll just spin right round, walk quickly towards me, push his nose right up to mine and we'll be face to face now, staring deep into each other's eyes and he'll shout "AND I THINK YOU HAVE A VIVID IMAGINATION, SIR!". And then there would just be a silence between us. And people nearby will have stopped doing what they were doing...and you would be able to cut the air with a knife and in the end I'd have no choice. I'd have no choice but to go up and just see Esther again. Get re-acquainted and just see how things pan out...and hope she doesn't want to go camping. *(Silence. He lays the noose on the table.)* But that's it. That's what I've been thinking about lately. That's what I worry about. *(Pause. He then picks up the noose. He goes and picks up the chair.)*

ESTHER. But that day Richard was crying on the sofa about old Tutankhamun was when the bubble burst. Too much had happened to get us there, I suppose, and we just couldn't let it go or fix each other. Its roots were rotten. With death. Of her, she died of course...and betrayal. Betrayal of Arthur. My Arthur. His Arthur. I could tell he missed him. That's how "we", came about. And Richard knew that as early as then, he really did. We pretended for a bit, sure, that we made the right decision, but it was just pretending. We were just, well, hollow, he and I. He got a job at the zoo near where

we lived and after a couple of months he would start to
bring home some of the animals at night. You weren't
allowed to do that. I even told him so myself. I said,
"You can't be bringing home the animals at night".
But Richard had an idea that he could train them to
do all kinds of things that you wouldn't imagine them
being able to do. You wouldn't believe some of the
things that he tried to get them to do but when they
finally found out that he was taking Paco home, one
of the chimpanzees, well he got sacked and then it was
just odd job after odd job after that. That's when, well
like I said, he, well there were no longer two hands
on the steering wheel. Let's just say that. *(Long silence)*
This is the Hollywood movie in my mind. I'm eighteen
again, back in the day, in another century. I'm just
finishing sixth form and I'm interested in rocks, let's
say. Geology. I don't know where that comes from,
I suppose I just like how they seem to last forever
and I want to go to Oxford and study all about that.
To better myself. A pipe dream maybe. Not many
girls at my school, in this sort of town, want to do
anything like that. My Geography teacher suggests I
should write something, a writing sample, you know,
something scholarly, to show those folks at Oxford
what I can do. And that's how I meet Arthur at the
local library. Of course old Mr. Huey is in charge at
the time, but on this particular day I come into the
library wanting to get my hands on something telling
me about sediment dispersion in Northumberland or
something like that. And young Arthur's behind the
desk on his own. Looking all handsome. Rumour has
it that if you're female, of a certain age and dogs don't
bark at the sight of you, the way you get out of paying
your fine for returning a book late if old Mr. Huey is
otherwise engaged, is to take a walk with young Arthur
over to the periodicals. The moment I first see him,
I know whatever book I'm going to take out, I'm not
going to return it on the date stamped! I take out the
maximum of six and I know I'm gonna keep them for

eight weeks longer than I should! Really build up a fine! Something I have to really work to pay off!

(**ARTHUR** *looks up at the ceiling. He looks up over to his right and then looks up over to his left.*)

ARTHUR. Halogen lights. That's what we have. All the years here, I should have…you can't hang anything on halogen lights. *(He takes a moment. He brings the chair back to the table, still holding the noose.)* There are three ways you can do this. The first is out of the question now. The one you may be familiar with. Just don't have the fixtures for it. I'm not complaining, mind. The lights we have in here served us very well. Those types of bulbs are quite economic. They last a long time. We had problems with them initially. We may have cut corners at first, we ordered cheap and the first batch we had gave off a buzzing sound whenever they were on. Which, in a library, well you can imagine. Distracting, disruptive and defeats the purpose. But depending on how well it goes, doing the drop, death should be instant. You drop. You break your neck. And that's it. The second way is vertical, just the same but without the drop. It's slower, you don't break your neck, you just crush your windpipe. But again. It's out of the question. Nothing to hang…like most things, it comes down to logistics. *(He puts the noose around his neck and he ties the other end to the leg of the table.)*

ESTHER. Meantime, I just start hanging around at the library whenever I can, trying to get up the courage to talk to Arthur. I'd read a couple of things, but most of the time, I'm just holding a book and looking at the words but Arthur doesn't know that, he just thinks I'm a quick reader. Anyway, one day all my loitering there pays off. He comes right up to me and asks me "So what do you think about Nixon?" "I've never been," I reply. I was just teasing him. I'm not even sure there's a place called Nixon. Arthur means the American President Nixon's resignation from the day before. I laugh anyway, and he laughs and he asks me out for dinner that night. Well things just seem to take on a life of their own after that and we're married the following summer. All this is after my first year at Oxford because guess what? I got in. Yes I did. And that's really how we seem to progress the two of us, me with my work and him and his library. There's no phone call to change things, no anthropology display, no Eskimos or museums. Me and Arthur, we have a family now, two boys, Alvin, after his dad, and John, after that actor in *Bergerac*, and we work hard but we just seem to never get sidetracked. It's kind of funny but that's the great thing about Arthur and I. We never let ourselves get distracted by anything but each other. So that's the Hollywood movie. A small town story. Daft, eh? Who thinks like that but me? Maybe it's a generation thing.

ARTHUR. When conditions don't allow for those first two. And that's what we're looking at here. Then you resort to the horizontal. See? *(He starts walking away from the table.)* …and I would just push away from it. Just a quick dash over there. *(The rope gets tighter.)* Just a quick dash…just start running this way and it'll be curtains. *(He keeps moving but stops when the noose seems to be getting tighter. It hurts.)* But I imagine that it hurts to high heavens. And it's just not for me. *(He unties the noose from around his neck.)* You think you've made the tough decision and then you have another just as bad. *(He unties the rope from the leg of the table and rolls it up. He puts it back in the sports bag.)* Thank you. But no, thanks. *(He reaches over and puts the matches and the petrol can back in the sports bag also. He addresses the two items.)* Thanks for everything. But not today. Thank you. *(Longer silence. Almost instinctively, he picks up the paracetamol and the bottle of water as if to take two again but decides against it. He puts the cap back on the paracetamol tub and puts it back in the bag.)* Those were just making me feel nauseous. *(Silence)*

ESTHER. "I have designs on you." That's what Arthur said to me that day. "I have designs on you. Come to dinner with me." Right after I made that dumb joke about Nixon. It was so nice. *(A beat)* I never did go to Oxford or anything like that. I know nothing about rocks.

ARTHUR. And the way they swarmed in yesterday. Just pushing and pulling books off the shelves and throwing them into boxes. Kicking them around, throwing them to each other, standing on them, with no respect for the order in which they stood. Most of those books had been where they were longer than they've even been alive some of them. They were laughing and joking and reading out titles that they thought were funny to each other. Saying their stupid jokes and all I could do was just sit there and watch. And think that they were nothing but bullies. Just... bullies. *(Silence)* I had a friend at school. Gordon. He was built like a barn. He used to just rough people up whenever he felt like it. Whenever he was bored, he'd just rough them up, that's what he'd do. Never did anything to me. Never laid a finger on me, but one day he got hold of a lad's bag. I don't remember the lad's name. Just snatched it right out of his hands and starts swinging it around, laughing and we were laughing too – because if you didn't laugh with Gordon chances were that he'd lamp you. So he keeps swinging this bag around and the young lad's begging him to put it down because it's got something inside it but Gordon just keeps laughing and swinging and throws the bag against the wall. The lad screams and runs over to his bag as if it was his dog or something that just hit that wall. He screams and everyone just laughs some more and I'm laughing too...and the lad's on his knees with his bag on his lap and he opens the bag up and takes out a chess set. A chess set. And now it has all these broken pieces...but it's not your regular chess set. It's like it's made of marble or something. Maybe not marble, that sounds quite posh, but something marble-like and it's expensive looking and old looking and this lad's crying about his broken chess set and whimpering softly about it not being his but that it was his dad's, his uncle's or his grandad's or something. It was pretty daft to bring something like that to school but this lad brought this thing to school. And the sight of this lad crying over a chess set just made everybody laugh more. Because it was a chess set and what a stiff for bringing a chess set to school, and not only that, but it's a boy crying. Over a chess set. On three counts it was funny to everyone who was watching. Well I felt like that kid did yesterday with all those Gordons jumping around the place. I wanted to say "Eh, just go easy, will you?"…but I think they would have just laughed and kept on throwing all those books around some more. *(He takes out a knife and a 9mm Luger from the sports bag and inspects them both. He feels the weight of each in either hand.)*

ESTHER. The last time I spoke to Arthur was the day Richard and I left. I mean, I tried. In those last twelve or fourteen months of me being alive and that, but he never gave me the chance. I understood. I did. At first anyway. Oh I sent letters, cards. No reply. I'd call the library and he would hang up, I'd call him at the house and the same. I'd drive up there when I knew he was home. I'd knock, stand there with my tail between my legs and wait but he would never answer. He'd just stand there behind the front door, I mean I could hear him, shuffling his feet, waiting for me to leave. That must have happened about six or seven times. The two of us just standing there for five minutes or so, just two yards apart, either side of what used to be our front door. Then one day, out of nothing really, I check the mail, an envelope I had self addressed and a card inside, the first thing I sent to him all those months ago about wanting to meet him. Arthur always was a little penny pincher, yes he was. Well I swear my heart just stopped. On the back in his handwriting it said …

ARTHUR & ESTHER. "For some reason I've been thinking about you lately. Perhaps the lake at sunset, next Thursday, might be appropriate."

ESTHER. He meant up at Angelzarke, where he and I had our first picnic together. Richard never went there. Not with Arthur and me anyway. It was always our special place.

ARTHUR. Well...not really much of a choice when you get down to it. One's bloody and violent. And the other's just the same but slower and you feel it. *(He puts down the knife. He holds the Luger at arm's length, careful not to point it at himself.)* I always thought it was a mistake in America when allowing the right to bear arms. Like building your house out of Play-Doh. Liberating and unique at first, but you should anticipate problems later. Still in some ways... I...er... *(He notices a solitary index card on the floor. He goes over to pick it up. He looks at it wistfully. He turns around slightly and takes a look around the empty space behind him.)*

ESTHER. Then two days later, I received divorce papers for me to sign. From his solicitor. Which after his card from a couple of days before was...well it was like a punch in the stomach. It would have been a lot to take at any time but after the card, well, you understand. I looked at the postmarks on both, the divorce papers and the card, and they were both mailed on the same date. He could have changed his mind about meeting me and had the papers sent after, I knew there was a chance of that sure...but blimey, solicitors aren't that quick. I just figured that maybe that process was already in motion when he had a change of heart and he did want to meet me to set things straight. To maybe start again. So I went there and I waited. Wait, wait, wait. But he was never once late for anything and he never did show up. And he would have known that I had the papers by then. So that was that. And once the sun set, that really was that.

ARTHUR. I never wanted any of this to sound like, like I'm
giving up. I know that's what it sounds like. I know
that's how people see people who do this kind of thing.
All my life, I've tried. I've tried to do the right thing.
And I feel like I haven't asked for much in return. And
apart from occasionally telling some of you to lower
your voice or be quiet, because it's distracting to others
who are reading, I don't think I – or I'd like to think
that – I haven't forced myself on anyone. Or told them
what to do. I sometimes wish I had stood up more. But
to tell you the truth, I thought my job, my livelihood,
what I chose to do – I never thought I would have to –
that I'd be pushed to that – I didn't take it for granted,
no. Not for a second. I've always respected the place.
When you open in the morning and close at night, you
can't not respect something like that. The one blessing
in all of this is that my father isn't alive to see any of
it. I can't imagine coming home to him last night and
telling him about how they stripped this place. It's
hard to comprehend that you're the last man standing
in your family. That you're the one at the end of the
line. I'm the last of the Deweys. We were like runners
in the relay race of life. Melvil, Godfrey, Alvin, Arthur.
They say a lot of things about my great-grandfather
but he was a brilliant man. There is no question about
that. *(Proudly)* He divided knowledge into nine classes,
and with each assigned them a numerical range!
"Philosophy – 100", "Religion – 200", "Social Sciences –
300" and so on. Right through to "Languages", "Pure
Sciences", "Technology or Practical Arts"…"Fine
Arts", "Literature" and finishing with "900 – History
and Geography". He also added a "Miscellaneous"
which started at 000. These were for General Works.
Like encyclopedias, that kind of thing. Each item that
comes under one of these disciplines, these areas
of knowledge, is assigned a number in that range,
called a class number. The logic is hierarchical: that
is, within a main class, there are various subdivisions
or subclasses, and these are divided, subdivided

further, getting more specific. So for example, we initially put *28 Ways to Terminate Your Existence and Questions You May Have* by Montgomery Swank in "100 – Philosophy/Psychology" and then further classified it in "180 – Personal Development", and within that in "189 – Death". After the three leading numbers, decimals can be used for as much further subdivision as needed, so "189.2 – Health through Thought", but then, when we go further "189.24" you'll find ways to kill yourself. We only had one book of that nature. Swank. That was it. But within the system there is a place for it! There always is! *(He relents slightly.)* Well I don't know if any of you followed all of that but those of you who did, I hope you realised something. He was a great man because what he came up with was more than a way of organising a few books, oh yes... more than a system of classifying a few things. He came up with something that was...and has become... why, a living and breathing thing! Don't you see? It's consistent. It adapts but it remains loyal. To the way in which it was created. It accommodates...it doesn't replace...or...or kick anything out...see, it has values. Integrity. Loyalty. Values you would want in a human being. Values that are...dammit, values that are going, and going fast from where I'm standing. See, he understood that everything had its place. There was room for everything and that's what we do. Libraries have room for everything. If you want it we can get it for you. There's a system in place, for order...but you can borrow it. We'll lend it to you. No charge. Not a penny. And anyone can join. Anyone. But share. Bring it back so others can read it, if no one wants it, you just renew! If everyone just had this Dewey Decimal mode of living there would be no need for any of this. It wouldn't come to this!

ESTHER. *(a fixed stare into the light, she speaks in a rapid tempo, a heightened sort of monotone)* Esther Margaret Huey of Lancashire, England. Maiden name Turner. It really wasn't meant to be like this. Happy child, lively teenager. Now far less happy. Far less lively. Summers when you were young. Family swims. Those who loved you. Making sure you didn't go under. Look at you now. Why aren't they here, wish they were here, or probably not, not to see this, either way, water's so cold it stings, feels refreshing, backpack, rocks, feels right. Picnic basket, full of pebbles, hangs around your neck, not a desired look but now in control and ready to roll. Face first or on your back? Face first or on your back? Face first, walk some more, wade some more, step, step, deeper now, much deeper, drop, didn't expect that, the end begins. No going back. In over your head, out of your depth, heavy, so, so heavy, pushing, pushing down, pulling you down, push – heavy again, very heavy, heavy, light, light now, light, feeling light, light, dark, darker, darker, black. *(Pause. She comes out of her trance. She's back. Brief silence)*

ARTHUR. I know how it must look. I do. Crazy guy with a gun talking bonkers and you're all just nodding along because you're scared I'll blow your head off. But I won't. I promise you that. I won't. I won't harm any of you. But it's not bonkers. Really it isn't. It's that weight that I carry. It's a double-edged sword. It has always been something to be proud of where I came from. A legacy that you inherit but it comes...with it comes a weight. A weight of achievement. A history. I suppose the choice comes down to who I am. Really. I suppose that's true for all of us. That's what we need to face. If I'm a Dewey. Which I am in blood. Then I've let the team down. I have. I can't even prevent a small community library being renamed an Academic Centre or "The Info Lounge"...or from having dozens of computers being installed...and turning half the place into a games arcade...or when they come and tell me that the space can be better served empty, to rent out for functions or sold as office space for business, I just have to take it. And sit by and watch them ransack the place. And I feel guilty. Because you think Melvil would have stood for that? You think he would have let that happen? You think anyone would have tried that on with him? He had respect. He had a name. He was a Dewey. He had clout. I'm not a Dewey. Not now. It's my blood but not me. I feel him though. I feel him watching and I know what he's thinking. He'd be watching right now and saying, "Go ahead. Pull the trigger."

ESTHER. You really do like to listen, don't you? I don't so much. My mind wanders. I may have reacted badly. I do get a little embarrassed talking about my suicide. You do, don't you? I was silly probably. Things move on and you'd eventually wonder, most likely, what all the fuss was. It's a funny one, but you just enter a zone where it's the only thing you see as a solution, as a relief, you know? But I mean, standing me up like that in such a gutless, cowardly way. I do think that about him. Not even being able to pick up the phone and tell me himself. Ignoring my phone calls, ignoring my letters. Standing behind the door while I'm knocking away. Twenty-nine years of service I gave that man. I lived my life, my happiness, my security, defined and determined by him. Nothing more than a passenger at times. And how dare he not come out that night and have the courtesy to hear me out. I may have made a mistake or two, sure, but I was Esther. I was *still* Esther.

ARTHUR. I'm my father's son when it comes down to it. He was a book bender. And pretended he was something he's not, yes. He was not a great man. Not one you would call "great". But he was a good man. His own man. A one woman man. A family man. A Huey. And I never heard him say a bad word about anyone. And he'd say, he'd say "Put the gun away…let it go." *(After a couple of seconds he puts the Luger back in the sports bag.)*

ESTHER. Life. What an enterprise. We were all very lucky to have had the chance, weren't we? Amazing really. You must have a story. You all look like you have a lot going on inside of you.

ARTHUR. You know, that lad came to school the next day. The day after his chess set was smashed. He came to school the next day. And the day after that, and the day after that, until we all finished. But I never learned his name and whenever I saw him, I couldn't look him in the face. I wonder if he ever thinks back to that day when Gordon threw his bag against the wall. *(Silence)* I need to do something. *We* need to do something… that's what I need to do. *(He takes out a shoebox with an alarm clock taped to it. In the shoebox is a bomb. He winds the alarm clock. It begins to tick. He places it on the table.)* Loyal patrons. Please exit through the main entrance. The library will be closing in fifteen minutes. Thank you. *(He sits. He stays. Lights fade to black on* **ARTHUR.** *A silence.)*

ESTHER. Life. Crikey. I mean, where do we go from there? *(A beat)* Well here, I suppose. But…but without forgiveness there's nothing. That's what I thought then and that's what I think now. And I forgive him. I forgive him for not forgiving me. But you have to forgive yourself too. And now, I suppose I do. Now I do. I forgive myself.

(A silhouette of a young man appears before **ESTHER** *as a warm light bathes the stage.)*

Arthur?

(The silhouette of a young man holds his hand out and gestures for **ESTHER** *to come with him.* **ESTHER** *briefly re-addresses the audience.)*

Thank you. Good luck. **(ESTHER** *goes towards the silhouette.)*

(Lights fade.)

The End